For George Stierhoff
 with best regards,
  Mary Cheever

Nov. 23, 1980

The
Need for
Chocolate
and other poems

THE NEED FOR CHOCOLATE
and other poems

by
Mary Cheever

STEIN AND DAY/*Publishers*/New York

First published in 1980
Copyright © 1980 by Mary Cheever
All rights reserved
Designed by Louis A. Ditizio
Printed in the United States of America
Stein and Day/*Publishers*/Scarborough House
Briarcliff Manor, N.Y. 10510

"Two Ducks" and "Green Heron" previously published in *Open Places*. "America, Bel Pensiero" and "November in the Arcadian Shopping Center" previously published in *Inprint*. "Eye of the Wrecking Ball" and "Elegy for a Courthouse" previously published in *The Croton Review*.

Library of Congress Cataloging in Publication Data

Cheever, Mary.
  The need for chocolate and other poems.

  I. Title.
PS3553.H34867N4   811'.54   80-5390
ISBN 0-8128-2728-7

For Fred, Ben, Susan,
and John

Contents

Dandelion	1
So Many Women Alone	3
The Need for Chocolate	5
Oh Susanna	6
Love and Death in the Beauty Salon	9
The Wig Dummies	12
Undinal	14
We Will Be Bound	16
Gorgon I.	18
Gorgon II.	20
After Dinner	22
It	23
Spring Song	24
A Passport and Other Pictures	25
Happy Birthday, Susie	30
Webs	33
Mother	35
Two Ducks	37
Green Heron	40
Thrush Song	42
Views of the Hudson	44
I. Bridging	44
II. America, Bel Pensiero	48
III. November in the Arcadian Shopping Center	49
IV. Driving to Congers	51
V. Man and Mountain	54

Eye of the Wrecking Ball	57
Elegy for a Courthouse	59
Wisteria Morning	61
English 53	65
A Knell for Teachers	68
The Girl Who Talked Too Much	70
Daffodils	72
The Rock and the Flower	73
La Coiffure de Mademoiselle Amdur	74
To Emily Dickinson in Heaven	75
Silverface	76
White on White	84
Skunk Glee	87
Earth Day, April 1970	88
Prospect Street	91
Remains	103
For All the Dead	106
American Cancer Society	107
This Is	109
New Hampshire Finding	110
How I Feel About Trying to Write a Poem About This Hill in New Hampshire While Staying on the Hill in New Hampshire	122
Sugar Maples	123
Blue Stone	127
To Alpheus Woodward Who Has not Shown up to Mow the Upper Field Which Once Belonged to his Own Grandmother	129

The Need for Chocolate and other poems

Dandelion

The dandelions were never fatter.
Uprooting, weedkillers by the hundred pound
Have only persuaded them to spatter
Yolk yellow further acres that were lawn
And then with seedheads thick on glossy stems,
To slaver them from end to end,
Their tooth-edged leaves submerged in foam,
While other vagrants on the pond
With trumpet honk and shout
Parade new gosling fleets around
Announcing spring's first throe is out.
Spring's first sunshine is spent
That in the village brought the old and sick
And lame and poor to step and pavement,
To bloom on porches that are blooming thick
With roses now, angelic opulence shocking
The vagrant eye; white roses flocking,
Red roses flaming and dropping, Peace

Strain roses big as babies' faces,
Pink and pale yellow fading to clay
Tan, rouge and bruise violet, impossibly
Beautiful as angels falling and dying.

Roses tell love; dandelions tell time,
And when the feathered clocks are blown
There will be stems enough to make a chain
All the way down to town and back again,
To curl and leave a bitter milk between
Your teeth, the lion's tooth, dandelion.

So Many Women Alone

Startled awake by the knowledge
Someone is staring
From the pillow beside her head,
Turned sideways the better to stare,
He is dead, then, she suddenly knows.

In that first autumn of his death
He found comfort in his own neighborhood.
To so many women in the big houses alone
His command was habit, the dogs would fawn,
The walls admit his slide, silent as sleep
Into their wide clean beds.

He is dead, then, she knows,
If this is he. Those are his eyes,
As always bright as glass,
Able to close no more
Than his poor staring mouth.

Although fleshless, he remained red
Indian brown and firm as a root
Under the frozen ground. The women
In echoing solitude, in regret
For their small refusals in the past,
Would not appear to him cold and unfeeling
Now, but bewitched, reached to his will
And took him in embraces close
And fond as memory, all through the days
While the bright leaves tarnished and fell
On the green spreading lawns,
Through the lengthening cold nights,
And through the rattle and stare
Of the bleaching, killing weather.

The Need for Chocolate

The need for chocolate or other sweets,
like liquor for some, drugs
or one sole lover more than any other—shrug
the question that has no answer: what makes one
person need another this way? Until the way is gone—
sweet mouthing and melting chocolate,
                              whatever you crave
as comfort or just desert, but should not have
because it rots the teeth or strains the heart,
learn to do without.
                       You have plenty of bread,
lockers of well hung meat,
loads of greens and green perfect fruits
trucked in from distant states.
Your need for chocolate is all in your head.
                            You think you want it.
You're better off without it. Break the habit.

Oh Susanna

Horsechestnuts are in flower, all white
but there at the corner one branch of pink,
a sport or the mark of an old graft.
The buds burst and the leaves and peaks
spilled out like pieces of a puzzle.
Now the white ciliate blossoms shine under noon.

Horsechestnuts were used for an ailment of horses.
The horse's skin was slit, the peeled nut inserted
"to draw the poison out."

A backing car nearly knocks into this station wagon,
a brass-green, broadass hardtop convertible.
Some sad frighty woman? No, it's a man.
The woman in a babydoll nighty moves at the kitchen
    door.
Recognition rocks into me, leeches on and through
to cramp my bowels with sweet sore memory.

I do not know the woman
but the roll of her hips and slant of her neck and
    thigh,
an indolent extended arm that dismisses her chores
show me she has newly bloomed a larger self
after a rooting in the loamy depths,
a dissolution on the peaks of pleasure
and now so brims, spills over treasure
that mere legal tender will tinkle and shine
like tourists' small change at her shrine.

Once I was content that joy
does not shine and shout.
I was wrong. It shines out
even in the noon shadow
of the flowering chestnuts.

I do not know the woman.
She is my neighbor. I could kill her.
She has diseased this day. Go home,
take aspirin, plenty of fluid and rest.

Oh Susanna,
on the great freeways you cannot walk.
You cannot drive to innocence or wisdom
in the family suburban,
or away from pain.

Love and Death in the Beauty Salon

                Prone
in a back room of the beauty salon
I look across the pale linoleum
at a vinyl glove holding a rolled up nylon
                              stocking,
into the rimmed and wrinkled opening
from which a hand hastily withdrawn
left the fingers last to let go
half inside.

                Three stump fingers
and a discolored thumb, pale and contorted,
the glove grasps as in rigor mortis
the diaphanous, delicately brown,
entirely passive, swooning
                          stocking.

A Norse
lordling abducts an Arab princess.
Overtaken on the river by a storm
the lovers perish, their drowned bodies
tightly embracing, are washed ashore.

                      Tonight
the cleaning woman will strain and mutter
stooping to remove this pale detritus.

                      This place is quiet.
Out in the paramedical arena
three young men dressed as Italian lovers
in flowered shirts, low belts and sideburns
greet the few joyless customers
with smiles and passionate eyes.
Are beauty parlors obsolescent
as maternity floors, movie palaces
and pavillions for tubercular children?

The stumpy glove fingers
sticky as my legs are
with depilatory wax
hump and clasp the stocking
in the corner of the floor,

as my legs remember
the touch of your hand,
my love, even in disaster,
in the moment of death and beyond.

The Wig Dummies

"The Daughters of Albion hear her woes
and echo back her sighs."
—William Blake

Pale, clothskinned heads, the wig dummies
lean gracefully, smooth and featureless
from their clamps. One takes for torso
the cabinet with brassy nipples in double rows.
One, in a wiglet, preens like a petted cat
under the hairbrush, then slips her socket
to ride on an arm to the sink.

From the separate necks,
circular sections capped with plastic,
I see dependent pale curved shoulders, backs
and hips, dressed by the blinds in slices of sun,
shapes heavy and tense as Blake's illusive women
hung forward from vague, massive knees, bent
on the pale tile floor, as noblewomen consent
to the guillotine.

                    Nearby in the broomcloset
organs, brains and livers, suitably spongy and pale,
wait among the detergent precipitants of mind
and the mystic spores of soul.

Undinal

There is an anthozoan,
A flower-animal, that man is host to,
Delicate as maidenhair fern, sensitive
As touch-me-not seedpods or sea anenome.

No one can see it
Until it moves to wither and contract
Clenching back to root
And followed so fast by scorn and spleen
That few can see it then.

Watch for it, maiden, mermaiden,
For only while it streams and grows
Upward in the ocean of his eyes
May you catch and swim the rayed plumes,
Those feeding, stinging tentacles,
And climb into air that is magical
To scale and strip and part you legs
And shape you feet to flee
Across the land, running free.

We Will Be Bound

Come live with me and we will join
long warm dim mornings
to our fractured nights.

Mornings while your sleep divides
our loving minds
by an easy opposite action
I will arrive
at the refrigerator
our union postulates
and over the stove
that by our love is given
I will subtract
from our white weeks
the fat light noons
and brew them black
and wash them white again.

Come live with me and we will mend
with long warm mornings
our disheveled nights.

Then will each stitching
catch us closer as the needle
pricks and latches
lifts and draws away to pull us fast
we will be bound to love at last.

Gorgon

>   "American woman
>   Stay away from me.
>   Mama, let me be.
>   I don't need your war machine.
>   I don't need your ghetto scene."
>   —The Guess Who

I.

I have sometimes complained, husband,
that as you feinted, shadowboxed and blindly
jived to that misty monolithic woman in your mind
I have been battered, drowned under your blows.

Not knives, not brassknuckles, not poison or needles,
no weapons, no holds between you two
were foul or out of bounds.

Now suddenly in the dawnlight
lying across our bed while you fuss
and nicker at my breast
I can feel myself growing.
I have become immense.
The shadows curve black from my body,
which is glowing moonwhite.
I am beautiful. God, how beautiful!

Dear, if you should decide to take
the gold rings out of my ears,
you will need the ladder.

I would help you if I could,
but my arms have turned to stone.

II

You hold me so high
I cannot follow what you do,
I only know it is a kind of dance.

                        You,
with your dark sparkle, you
were always so quick to touch and kiss.
                      Who
are your partners now?

Worship is part of fear,
means to placate,
admits hate,
and you are right,
your rites obscurely recognize
my niceboned power, generations'
use and choice.

Look!
even in this afternoon,
our handsome children grown and gone,
I am magnificent,
my arms and legs, my neck, full columns,
my profile still fine cut.

     Only my eyes—
do not look in my eyes.
Who searches there
earns my rockslide talk,
my stony exclamations,
or sees the hurt
of your fickle ministrations,
your life-denying husbandry.

     Husband,
this is my act of love,
to be your shield.
     Hold me aloft.

After Dinner

Like paddles, or windmill blades,
Toes up, head back
Then down again, they rock.
They are gray,
Their features bluntly sketched,
Eyes, nose, mouth, shoetips.
They have a lot to say
To one another and to anybody else
Who may be listening.
They call for leadership
And praise control, each one secure
On his own pivot and earned perimeter.
They rock and talk and stroke the quiet air
And land, soft as a woman and so pretty
In her hills and flowering fields
But always so preoccupied with the affairs
Of day and night, seasons and atmosphere,
She does not follow their strict mathematics
Or windy travel.

It

There are so many things you can do with it.
You can back it into an empty shell
And wobble along in the shallows waving a pincer,
Or work it down to a riddle cut with rhymes
And sell it to strangers,
Or wear it around your waist like a lure
Or a sneer,
Or let it go up like grease in the smoke
Or down like grease in the water,
Or you can ride it and stretch up a sail
And drive down a rudder and keel.

Spring Song

Trees are
Putting on Big Lash
Rolling misty skies.
Somebody's thumbing my buttons
Fumbling my skull screws. I
will crack like a tulip in
Bees' frying.

Scrim Scree Scry
Spring's coming!

A Passport and Other Pictures

A Birthday Poem for Ben

Looking for my passport
I found yours in the drawer, Ben.
This is the passport that you didn't want;
you didn't want to go, U.S. rich boy
on vacation, to the Caribbean.

In the picture
your hair is long over your forehead.
Your big man's shoulders
slump. You seem to draw
mist and shade from every state
and country of your mind
around you, hiding as you sometimes did
under the bed or in the woods.
Your full frank lips hang blank.

Only your look, aslant,
acknowledges to the camera's mirror eye
a possible shared amusement
or dislike.

When you were being born
I saw a red sun slip
from the white bottomless vault
of what I was and still must be,
that place lit white
where I have been
often but have not seen since.
Your sister spoke there
Like a wakeful bird over water
to greet you and to make
that dream of generation actual
as everyday park pavement
and every evening boiled egg suppers
in the kitchen all those early years.

In that longer confinement
I strained to read
all that I was and wished to be
in your face as I held you and rocked
singing to send you to sleep,
until in some late one of those too trivial
ordeals—in the cell and stocks
of the childsized room
and furniture, in steam
that curled the paper from the walls—
at last the tissues broke
and fell, I saw and knew that all
I seemed to suffer for your sake
was not for you but for some small
mistaken selfdom of my own.
At last I saw you, Ben.

Were you misnamed?
In the Bible, Benjamin
is Jacob's last and youngest son
as you are not, or have not been
since Fred was born.
Benjamin in Hebrew means
son of the right hand.
The hand I hold out to the world,
my wife and work hand, citizen hand
that pays and votes and writes,
is the agent and the port
of my smaller, shallow part.
A darker depth and broader sea and land
is represented in my left, my other hand.

This verse and others are the history
of that, our common country,
our shared Canaan. I try
and so far fail to sing out right
to the world the anthems of our nation
and commonwealth.

Birthdays, too, we share.
You were the present of my thirtieth,
the gift, present, past and future
of the power
both to be and see
myself in someone else. Yours to me, Ben,
mine to you, your passport, citizen
son.

Happy Birthday, Susie

Dear Susie, Susan
(that name I never quite believed we gave you),
I've counted out this birthday is your twenty-eighth.
My looking glass assures me it is so.

Here are some sentimental resurrections.
In the first sketch the figure
billowing off the stool is Faith,
whom you have engaged in difficult discussion.
She has been passing on the word
according to Father Divine.
It is easy to see the word is being contested
and also easy to see who is winning.
These are sketches from life.
Above, on the windowsill is a pot of chives.
And would you have remembered that the kitchen
    stove

on 59th Street stood on legs—Regency, Queen Anne?—
bowed, tapered and pawed, with just the suggestion
of an abstract claw? How could we forget
that under it we lodged the Brearley Science rat
very unhappily one Christmas vacation?

Before the rat, or Brearley, you had another pet.
We met him first when you put down your telephone
one day and announced, "The lion is busy."
He was not abstract.
When he was sitting on the velvet chair from Sloane's
only you could go near it.
You had to struggle to hold him on the leash
when you walked on Sutton Place,
but he would always stop for ice cream at Boots
    Pharmacy.

Along with these old sketches, Susie,
I have three wishes for you on your twenty-eighth:
first, may you always have plenteous faith;
second, may you never stop questioning
and often be triumphant in discussion;
and third, and most important,
may your lion always be busy.

Webs

In many lights
the web appears perfectly transparent
but the finely woven
sticky threads grow in a cone
that holds and magnifies a white
like ancient suns,
its bright particularity
dazzling out all darkness.

Earth creepers when they reproduce
secrete a silk or ductile gut
to spin these tents of dense warmth
and keep them mended snug and taut
until the young fall out
to their own spinning.

The first supporting threads,
although lost or buried,
as the new tissues strain and sway,
through every filament relay
electric urges to the spider brain.

We love and weave. Steady weaving
binds like loving.
                        Webs torn or cut
tatter and catch a bitter soot
and pile into unlit spaces
and drop dark meshes
in our eyes and faces.

Mother

              of pearl is the inner layer
of certain shells. It is iridescent and appears
to be as soft and deep as it is smooth.
              Tip the shell. The mother of pearl
seems to slide like oil in a spoon.
If the outer shell is scraped or worn, the mother
of pearl will curve up over the rim
as drops of syrup roll and meet
on the rim of a spoon and fall in a solid sheet
when the syrup is ready to jell.
              Living
mother of pearl is a feeling
like a fluid slowly rising to a boil,
a fluid like syrup or milk or oil.

                              Living
mother of pearl is unsolid and volatile.
If it is not contained,
the mother of pearl will rise and roll
over the rim of the shell
and spread and sheet every jagged, painful,
wrong and ugly thing in the world
until it is covered cold and solid
and still as beautiful mother of pearl.

Two Ducks

Two ducks move
In identical grooves
Twin citrus sections
With one direction.

Look, both
Are sailing north.
Look back,
A double tack
Has swiveled them south.

S and a pillow
Pushing out yellow,
He billows,
She follows.

Two curled tail feathers
On the drake
With his grander inches make
His elegant only dress
For maleness.

While she leans and squawks her rage
At underwater menace
He maintains the steady pace
And stately carriage
Of marriage.

Wild geese and mallards
Earth and leaf colored
Swathe and slide
The water wide
But these two watch-me whites
Capture the light
Click the lake small
And chock it full
Of noise
Like wooden toys.

Green Heron

He putters or stalks rock still
at the pond's edge until
surprised he zigzags
like an old person
picking up parcels,
then, head feathers ragged,
with a squat and boost
takes flustered flight
as though he grabbed the first
bus to come along
sure to be sorry later on.
His russet crooked neck
tucks in angling the long bill
straight front like a funny nose.
His legs hang down
like lengths of yellow rope
frayed at the ends.

Like an iron gate he protests
as his "typical heron flight,
a steady wing beat,"
takes him out of sight.

Oh, my friend, fright does not become you
and my pursuit seems hopeless.
I have your likeness
neat on a glossy page
below your kin, the fabulous Great Blue,
sedately lifting your small crest,
spreading your lesser plumage.
Is this the best my love can do?

Thrush Song

There is such a thing
as too much thrush song
ringing, pealing, thrilling
in your ears, when you're alone
in a wet season, ringing
every quarter of the horizon.

reeahoo ooahree tweehor vareehee

rings in your ears
"does so rinse and wring/The ear..." Brother
 Hopkins.
That was before washing machines
except the kind
with a roll-wringer stuck on the side.

wet reeooreeoo treeooree oreepo

wet wet wash wring
ring roll gnash
gush tumble spin
all your sheets, fine garments, workwear, linens,
all your synthetics, dripdries, delicates,
Baby's clothes,
your daintiest underthings.

Views of the Hudson

I
Bridging

This cold April, dividing our counties,
    The wide river glitters
That fell in our first war from French Champlain
"Straight at the heart of the English colonies,"
    Last long reaches in the portage chain,
Muttering night canoes.

At the Hook, sails wait for the wind,
              wait for the tide.

That wooded ridge behind Hook Mountain's tail
    From Congers, where you are,
Is mined out flat as an opera set
From *Flying Dutchman* dusty thunder rolls
    To *Götterdammerung*, and altering powers
Litter both our shores—

Sail, bridge, reach over as the river alters.

Engines scrapped, castles crossed or fallen, the ferry
    Beached for the bridge's gray
Equations: windshield and mirror: G.M., steely mother,
Steams out, stackbristled, on her glistering fry
    As Hook across the Zee
His scarred head leans away.

Wait for the wind, wait for the tide.

From Dunderberg, the mothballed ships
    Have dropped downstream, frail
Liberties at sea again, but Bell
And Con Ed send more leggy, necklaced heralds up
    and down and tall steam plumes
At Haverstraw mark new power mills.

Sail, bridge, reach over as the river alters.

At Indian Point derricks cross the sky, attending
    Fission reactors,
Bulbs paired beneath a bulb-tipped shaft preparing
Potent emissions, male necessity
    Built huge in jealousy
Of the mountains and the fertile river water.

Wait for the wind, wait for the tide.

Over the earthfault, shield and mirror
    The river flows and blooms.
The red lava lip chilled to a flaking wall
Up this long reach falls in your hills in Rockland.
    Some gods still play at quake and weather
Mooning like white stone sunk in the green wetland.

Sail, bridge, reach over as the river alters.

Now from both shores the aerial towers send
    Red signals over.
Be side to my side, hand to my holding hand, friend
On the far side of the river that covers
    In silt the old channel, in bright tidewater
Breeding and changing, the earthbreak, the old division.

II
America, Bel Pensiero

Broadway to the Highlands arcs the dock radials,
Drops, climbs, where scaled house faces pin
Wheels of streetlight and leaflight, evergreen
And sycamore, to the slow riding river hills.
Old Sing Sing Hollow settlement backs to the
    truckfalls
A new Italian stucco and shingle skin,
Around the blackened mills and steepwalled Kill,
Stairwell, arch and courtyard wedging a paesino
Of terrace and narrow garden plot, staked tomatoes,
Carparts, roses, stacked concrete blocks,
And, under loose planks, a teetering storm window,
A houseside fencewire leaning in ragged lilacs,
In the blue gloom, coin-bright, a net of moons,
The plumed horns, white Leghorn chickens.

III
November in the Arcadian Shopping Center

A conference of oaks over High Meadow
Apartments recalls Massaccio's fresco
of apostles robed in rose and umber,
St. Peter paying the tax collector.

That was James Speier's hill and wood
walled miles around where his mansion stood
that's burned and fallen.

So much sky
lifts over the shopping center
split with jet thunder
tossed with seagulls from tomorrow's weather,
you can hear the hinge of winter grate,
see winter's lid
catching as it falls
under the turning planet,
a blaze of copper, blood red,
gold and smoldering pale lead.

Stay,
calls the wide plaza,
under the wide sky and the apostolic oaks,
Stay, spend, look, this is Arcadia,
summer's promise, the arctic rumor,
the cold and pallor and dreadful clamor
of falling silver, copper and lead.

IV
Driving to Congers

Driving to Congers under
your white blue skies
something is pulling me
under like a river current
or the back of a wave.

I'm afraid of fire and drowning.

Something is dying under
your white blue eyes
leaving a shell like a cat smile.
Could I lick it away or couple
onto it like a length of hose?

I'm afraid of fire and drowning.

So much white blue kindness
spills out of your eyes
over the cat smile, the river
spills over the roads.
I'm afraid I'll blaze too high
and shatter like shale.

I'm afraid of fire and drowning.

The river is spilling over. I'm
still getting lost on Lake Road
missing the Congers corner
driving out over water
past the naked back
of the broken mountain.

I'm afraid of fire and drowning.

Something is driving me under
your white cold skies
leaving a song like a cat smile.
Could I lick it away
or fasten onto it like a rope
or a length of hose?

I'm afraid of fire and drowning.

V
Man and Mountain

For William Schuman

Far down the river where the shores
dissolve in haze, the city floats out
shocking into ragged towers the colors
of rock and sky. In my charmed memory
a man is a tower alive in every stone.

West across the bay, Hook Mountain,
hump and dome belling his hills along
stills wind, holds against slides and quarries
and pulls to his lip the shining river song.

Mountain is father to city in our story.
The god comes down from the mountain
or the god heard on the mountain sends a man
to build his temple on the plain.
A man is a tower alive in every stone.

Men make images of man, pillar and arch,
vault and tower, and in their hands
wood and metal voice delight and pain
spiriting a city out of stone and sand.

A man is a tower alive in every stone
risen in place, smoothly paired and bound
in suspense and sentience, every molecule
continuously measuring the powers around
in sonorous alarms and hallelujahs.

Hook holds his power, great bullbear, predator,
pain asleep, he gathers west my days.

As to the mountain, to the man I come
from lower ground, under stone, over water
easily, in well-remembered ways.

Eye of the Wrecking Ball

I ride the wrecking ball,
signal to the driver down in the derrick cab
to aim the ball right
at the old beams and the marble sills
and the heavy carved cornice.
                    I hold on easy
straddling the cable,
boots flat on the flat top of the ball
as it splits the high shell of this theatre
that was here before moving pictures.
                      I know my work well,
keep my grip and balance when the derrick lurches
swinging the cable wide.

              I stand in the sky
below the sixteen white wooden turrets
on the steeple of the Baptist Church
              over Main Street
that runs down steep to the depot
the river and the chipped, peaked hills
climbing the other side.
              I stand in the sky,
the derrick's eye, eye of the wrecking ball.

Elegy for a Courthouse

Before you see it you breathe it,
stonedust raised by the demolition.
All over downtown White Plains
there's an odor of tombs, of cold ruins.

Behind the boarded Main Street face
the busy wrecking ball and shovels
crawl and slam. Two great walls, one
pale paint patched, one gray stone,
worked, dentated, crowned, stand roofless,
free as Stonehenge, the sheer
size of them crying out Lear
madness, booming the Beethoven
Emperor finish. Colossus toppling,
the old courthouse is coming down.

As it goes, the elder courthouse,
built to walkers' scale of rougher stone
yellowed like an old tabby sits alone
neat as a nut unshelled, compact
complete and decorous, holding close
within it our father century
like virtue, like righteousness.
Shabby bishop of the law, the wreckers
have knocked his miter crooked now. Already
the eyes are broken.

Wisteria Morning

Goodbye to Briarcliff College
For Megan and Lynda

It's midMay again.
This is the week of wisteria mornings.
The purple beam searches in through the glass
as I move through the house.
Without warning it searches into my eyes.

The sun grows hot.
The wisteria is ahum. Fat bees nuzzle it.
It smells like Mum cream deodorant.
Walls of it thrill like a sentimental vaudeville number.
The girls come down the stairs in hoops and picture hats.
The baritone in tails stands in the spotlight.
Scarlett O'Hara is all laced up for the ball.
It's spring at Bloomingdale's.

The clusters fall in tiers of sixes and nines
from the teacolored leaves and the searching vines.
Before the last open the first have whitened and drop.
Each opening floret lifts a standard petal.
Vertical darker lips wing over the stamen purse
and the staminal tube that leads to the honey sack.
Floret hoods become flags, sails for the purse keels,
ads for the goods, bee bull's-eyes.
Each one has a lighter center and downy track.
The bee grasps the lips and balances on the keel
and places the yellow spot on the top of his head
on the yellow eye and probes the honey sack.

It's midMay again.
Megan and Lynda and Susan and Betsy have set out their
    pots.
The sun shines into the studio window
on plates and bowls and jugs and boxes and bottles,
slimnecked or widenecked and corked, squat and tall,
round and angular, smooth and scored, thrown and
    pinchpot,
mahogany, gunmetal, verdigris, blue.

Megan has made a wisteria purple teapot
with holes for a handle and a matching flatbottomed
    cup.
She has made more pots this semester than poems.
Pots and poems both may be useful and beautiful.
Both may hold time. Some hold a long time.
Like a pot a poem is easily lost.
A poem once found can never be broken.

It's midMay again. I will not see May here again.
Nor will Lynda or Betsy or Megan.
It's midMay again. I wake to wisteria morning.

English 53

Standing before you I can only guess
at what you see. For rare
moments when you give me back
a living image, I endure these others
when your faces slick as glass,
lit by incredulity, darkened by disgust,
fuse in one backward mirror
                       and I remember
ghostly grammarians
with rusty teeth and crumpled paper skin,
one mademoiselle's black bearded armpits
and complex corset under flowered voile,
                    her smell
more foreign than her mincing syllables,
sour and secret as strangers' closets,
strangely obscene

                  and a fräulein
round as a bottomweighted doll balloon
with flat mongoloid eyes and spit
threading on her lips, teaching German
translated into French, translated into kindness
and into love.   Students, pupils,
the love a teacher feels is cool.
Know it by this, it is as cool
as mirror glass that warms and lights
only in your reflections caught
by the strange fire that animates
as it consumes.

I stand before you,
Barbara, Constance, Val, Dolores.
Your faces darken, fuse and close.
The circuits short, the gears
clutch and grind rust.
Wet prickles my body hair and threatens
the papery skin around my eyes.

Whichever way you push me I will lean
lurch and stagger back at you again
or you can put me out or close me in
like something misplaced in a closet,
                        wasted and unclean.

A Knell for Teachers

Teacher, teach me a stone
A shell to sing and a wishing bone
And a tower rising out of the sea
Where the buoys are tolling rings for me.
Teach me a catch and a stitch to spare
And a ribbon to tie up my bonnie here.

Ring around a rosie.

Teacher, please teach off the grass.
Your "attempts to open an intercourse
With the world" keep you spinning on the black
Way out, way out, and don't come back
Till you've circled Mars and sung the runes
On the back of the moon to heavenly turns.

Ring around a rosie
There's another ring in hell.

"Telling lies to the young is wrong."
Add one right and get two wrongs.
The lies increase in the swarming shoal.
Cold and deep the truth lies still.
You're only wrong once so come and play
Ring around a rosie while you may.

Ring around a rosie
There's another ring in hell.
Hark, now I hear it, ding dong dell.

The Girl Who Talked Too Much

Did you ever notice
The difference in our ages
Is only a few days?

        —No.

Your mother and my mother
Mine in Brooklyn, yours in New City,
Were going around sticking out,
Yours with you, mine with me,
At the same time.

        —No.

Your father said to your mother,
Give us a kiss. . . .
My mother said to my father,
The grass is wet. . . .
Maybe the very same night.

My father said to my mother,
That would be great.
Your mother said to your father,
I forgot.

Suppose your father
said that to my mother
Or mine to yours . . .
Then what? Give us a kiss.

        —No.

Daffodils

Face to the yellow daffodil
face, a girl sighed,
      Oh, to be
so fresh, so pure, so all-
at-once! and put out coded
point on point of yellow light,
full throat and, flute by flute,
sweet lip and shining eye
                  and was.

The Rock and the Flower

For John Dirks

"See me, see me," cries the flower,
spreading its petals like the fingers
of drowning women, thrusting its yellow
center toward the sun, stripping
its petals back until they shrivel and fall.

The rock glistens in sunlight,
colors in rain, preens under snow,
takes moss, takes ice, shelters
the roots and green leaves
of the crying flower.

La Coiffure de Mademoiselle Amdur

A Long Faculty Meeting, an April Afternoon

Absence of light does not define
The black of Marianne Amdur's hair
Nor does its darkness seem the sign
Or cloak of shame, the social fear.
Rather it tells Scheherezade's nights
For here the strands in thousands shine
Amber and red netted with finer lights
like gemfire. They lift, fall, then join
Close black again to sweep a courtesy.

This black is a gloss on bright, color defined,
A whole society of light. Beauty
May be momentary in the mind
of Marianne, and black infernal
But in her hair it is eternal.

To Emily Dickinson in Heaven

Last night I had a dream
that seemed to show me
twenty or more persons
young and old can lie naked
side by side in a single bed
each one believing he or she alone
wants to make love.
I sent a hand out to explore my neighbor
and though what I felt was disappointing
his answer was ready and lewd: Oh, yes,
of course, but it can be dangerous,
he said, cocking an eyebrow
at invisible authority.
They say when this sheet
goes out to the laundry
the first wash water would feed and freshen
a herd of dairy cows. So we joked
and talked like kinsmen met a night
scarcely adjusted in the tomb.

Silverface

I

My friend Grace
calls her analyst Dr. Stoneface
because he is her fixed excuse
for telling, the rock on which she mills
and weekly spills her mindfall.

     Dr. J. William Silverberg
(berg for mountain, silver for river)
I call Silverface for mirror.
Whatever may be undone or askew
he shows me and returns to me
the very waves I radiate
then turns me out
bathed and aglow in my own light.

My gratitude
revives the platitude
that learning to love myself
I learn to love others as well.

Silverface, silvercool
mirrorface, mirrorfool.

Silverface, I cross your palm
with silver. Do you predict a calm
or perilous voyage? Will I find success
in a new business?
And the dark stranger I must meet
may he not come for many years yet?

Silverface is my doctor, not my friend. Grace
is my friend. She calls her doctor Stonyface.

Silverface, silvercool,
silverforce, am I silver's fool?

II

My Cape Cod grandmother
had tacked high on the bare weathered
boarding of her summer cabin,
in elegant embellished manuscript,
this legend:
> WORK IS PLEASURE

Was that a promise,
> Grandma,
>> or a threat?

Dear Dr. Silverface,
here with you
that order seems reversed;
you work, I pay,
together we fret
and labor
both for my good and better
                                leisure.
And guess what?
                Grandma,
                          this work is pleasure!

III

I play worlds
puzzling the pieces
filling the interstices
making your worlds
and crossworlds.
                      I play
I protest, I digress
dreaming new orders and degrees
on your hierarchal pyramid
until it overtips and slides
into circles that whirl away.

I make the worlds
            you twirl
like a circus seal
            on nose
and shoulder
and deftly toe around
under you.
            Your nods
your quick salutes
keep them aloft
            and turning
crossing and shining:

dollarworld, powerworld
mindworld, famegameworld;
Board, Jewry, Episcopation,
bench, eldership, corporation;
gear   pivot   jewel
rod   ratchet   wheel
worlds in commerce and collision
ticking and turning.

Gimbel gamble guggendale
rocketeller rosenvelt
osler flexner morgandollar
Gouldman Sochs Achsincloss
Barlew Bartuch Bachensen
Shlepstein, Schlitz, Lipperschitz
Silverfisch, silverburger, silverklutz.

Juggle them, bubble them all away.

Silverface, owleyes
                take off your specs
stir your spindleshanks
and naked as Adam and hand in hand
together we'll go back
into the garden to look for the snake.

White on White

We make a sort of art museum way
around ramps gently
up and up and gently down.
The objects of our search
and scrutiny rustle
or explode to life ahead
and behind us, dead
stable only in the instant
of encounter.

Through stages,
ages of white on white
we must paint all over
white canvases housewall high
to letterpaper small, then neat
and regular as clock ticks touch,
cross, figure, flake and petal cover
them with finicking light brushfalls
before we can begin to know how much
was there to start with
and how much we brought.

Content with circumspection
we play out the metaphor,
footnotes on the poured concrete,
until at last we come to an event
of importance, or what looks like one,
in newsprint black with a hint
of freshly dried blood,
vigorously brushed, apparently
inevitable and deeply significant.

So this is why we came
and how we go, we sigh then,
satisfied, and turn
to make our exits
gentle, multiple, final
as flake and petal fall.

Skunk Glee

For Mimi Glazer

Fur balloons
     in tiny tennis shoes,
          the raccoons
roll in and out of the lamplight
     scooping up Mimi's tidbits
         one by one
with dainty prosthetic mitts
       but pause, sway
and thoughtfully bow away when
       turning his inky
snake head, looping his plume tail,
       a skunk
figure eight rampant on dancers' tiptoes
       absolute
ruler of smell, executive of stink,
refreshes their memory.

Earth Day, April 1970

What shall we do with Mrs. Howley's bones?
Are they degradable? Can they be
consumed, recycled, burned?
I read she died last week, near a hundred
"years young," visiting at the home
of friends in Arizona. Our old headmistress,
                                      fright,
when you and I were twigs.
                                        Her bones?

Even then, one windy recess,
some child had seen her wig
aslip and from its net-tight nest
shine out, "little low heaven," her white
skull, the secret terrible apex
of her red flaring neck.

The red rage how it seized her,
                                  compressed
and rocketed her words,
which, declaiming evil, became the evil
                                  we had only guessed.
"Parasite! Pander! You pander yourself!"
                                  shaming
our sly encounter at the watercooler,
filling those paper cups with thick
pollutants. Pander? What could it mean?
Our potty, "body waste," or sex, "the nasty trick"?

Now only her bones complain.
                                  Or you!
You were her familiar.
Together we heard her tall son—
I had dreamed he was my sweetheart—
squatting over the funnies in her parlor,
richly fart.

Oh, what shall we do with the bones
of the Howleys, mother and son?
Will they settle into the river?
Will they sink in the wheely weeds?
Could we grind them into a meal
or set them in concrete,
then piously raise an artifact
in some garden spot or lot
left vacant for recreation,
a shape of words or junkyard steel
to rust and range the sky,
to hold and hail the white secret rage
of waste that will not die?

Prospect Street

On Prospect Street when I was born
tall maples held new redflocked veils across
a prospect of illusion raised in stone.
All that had seemed grandest in the past
in grander mass was simulated on that quiet hill
in clashing university. A castle
where languid boys took Physics
hunched glum defenseless battlements
against a neighbor pink brick
ducal palace so colossal
it would have flipped St. Mark's
into the Grand Canal.
Downstreet a lighter Italian fantasy
lodged Mathematics, and Zoology
in a hulking cloister hugged the corner.
An elegant small Greek revival mansion
behind all these soberly survived, still housing
archaic Hillhouse, patriarch turned recluse
furious over his dollars.

There was a legend
he had cut the sleeve from a workman's coat
because it hung on his side of the hedge
and on our way to school we passed that spot
in terror until we reached the open fields
that had been Hillhouse Farm, called Sachem's Wood
after another chieftain who was long gone.

When it grew too dark
for giant steps or hide and seek
we would dare to lie down flat
in the middle of the street
and look up into night
or press our cheeks
against the warm macadam
and listen to the blessing trees
and hear the streetcar
turning at the corner.

Large trees that were not woods,
large space, not fields, the backyards,
still stable rich and richly seasoned
by giant trees distending vascular fans
to heart that air; lax hedged and footloose fenced,
sloped down from Prospect to the deference
of narrower streets. We heard the backstreet shouts
distant and hoarse. Someone had chalked
  CHITE CHITE
on the board fence at Edwards Street corner.
        Italian?

       In that wide quiet,
the women resting, mistresses like maids,
dreamed foreign titles, license their first fathers
had decried, and into that dream gel Cotton Mather's
Satan, "always a small black man"—Oh, Sheik
of Araby—could slide like satin sleekly turning

the odor of longing to a powdery reek
like ten cent incense burning and favorite
fat lending library novels and stacks
of dusty comics and *True Romances*.
Exotic equaled erotic. To you, familiar spirit,
old fiend, what credit? That slot was ready made.

Sachem, when I had swung the wire gate
on Edwards Street, schoolday afternoons,
addict to fix, I walked into your woods.
In sagging bloomers and sprung mocassins,
I could be Robin Hood, Isolde cut
from Tristram by his own stern sword,
Theseus setting sail for Crete
or a brown bear warm in his winter sleep.
And when I had climbed to Prospect Street
and walked between the walls and towers,
I felt the pain of their distorted power
but never saw them. They were only real.

                    Real as my father's friends
and enemies: trustees, professors,
matrons, bankers, patrons, neighbors:
Trumbulls, Burnleys, Townsends,
Everits, Winslows, Seymours. . . .
None of them ever walked in Sachem's Wood.

"Good afternoon, young lady, and who are we?"

Who are we? Who was he, this monster grownup
in a place where no one left the paths but dogs
and children and in the spring the squatting
blackshawled women digging dandelions? Italians.

He teetered over me, vest-buttoned, mufflered,
thick-coated, sissy-rubbered, a chart
of haberdashery, all its craft
shrouding him from the moist spring air

up to a point high on his skinny neck
where the stiff collar expelled a face
puckered as last Saturday's balloon
and gentian-veined, the blister cheeks
dusted with bricky rouge. He raised his hat
from his careful crimson hair and grinned.

"What little girl are you? Indeed?"

                                      Whatever I replied
he did not hear. His red gaze raked the slope
on Sachem side and where it fixed
a fresh intrusion shocked the landscape.
Flitting around the Gothic dinosaur
of Peabody Museum tower,
this one was ample lady-shaped and draped.

Everit Noone, Everit Burnley Noone
was making moonshines, making monkeyshines
with sappy old Miss Bush.

He squirmed and giggled like a shameful girl
flushing a red that turned the brickdust pale,
trembled and threw a gloved hand up to wave,
then stifflegged out to Whitney Avenue
toward high-minded Cynthia's bugle call
I knew would skim an octave up and down:
"Everit, Everit, *dear*
Everit!" Just in time for tea.

Matilda, love, sweet Matty,
I've left a letter in the hollow oak.
I'll think of you at five o'clock
until five-thirty. Think of me.

Another afternoon, Miss Bush
loomed up on me as if to speak
but did not, did not lower her look
from the sunset flush on Prospect's towers.
A ribbon tugged her hedge of faded hair
and rattled on her ruffled palisades
in the same local storm that shook
her crooked umbrella and her pocketbook
and tinkled the buckles on her galoshes.
Her smile, as wan as winter leaves
and gaseous sweet, said, I am sweet Matilda Bush
and Everit, Everit Burnley Noone loves me.

Oh, Everit
I dreamed I burst
in small pale blooms
beside your warmth.
Love, I want to take your hand
and show you where the swallows
flicker low and fiddle ferns
thrust up their furry crooks
and violets crowd among the rocks
like little girls in sunbonnets,
our little boys in blue.

When the curving cry of the streetcar broke
with a spit and lurch onto Prospect's tracks,
who would be riding on the wicker seats?
Bad Mr. Nobody, cross Mrs. Maybe with swollen feet
and brown paper parcels, big girls and boys
herding and honking, awkward as geese
newly bewitched into human flesh.
And what could we see on our way downtown
across the Green to the five and ten and the movies?
New Gothic mammoths and their gray grandsires,
fat white Woollsey, domed like St. Peter's,
and the long brown arm of the cemetery.
The sentence those portal fingers held
was out of sight, a long block west
from Prospect Street: The Dead Shall Be Raised.

The tide that was receding then is out;
old Prospect is all retrospect, a hill
of clinkers, shells and pale refuse.
Saarinen's turtle has swallowed Seymour's
and two Victorian neighbor houses. In ours
gone flaky gray as hornets' paper, dentists
have swarmed and combed and crammed it wall to
    wall.
Hillhouse fields, cropped, are apartment shocked.
The Physics castle has hatched a cyclotron
housed rocket-high for dalliance
with the moon and other extraEarth romance.

(Two voices)

I never saw the tryst	Pale shoots
of those old lovers	whorl
ghost or flesh,	under the
but though	rocks
returning tides wash	skunk cabbage
Prospect	breaks
into West Rock	the ground
and push	like speckled
East Rock	snails
into Long Island	new leaves light
Sound,	the red maple
Everit	dangles
and Matilda meet	the oaks spit
and will meet	petal white.

      again
        for he
          was her ardent god and she
              was his green tree.

Remains

For my sister killed by a train

My mother said, Come here.
She had no body on,
only her head
walking on hair.

Mother, I fall for you
through a brown slick of photographs:

>Bride full lavish
>lace sails, fat
>roses dropping

>Babies slipping
>her arm like sleepy
>fish

I fall to the hill room where
bone thin and brown as earth
you raise again the body of despair
and pain.

Sister, I know your scream
from the shouting train's,
your eyes from the light eye
jumping the track
to knock me falling
out into night space after you
calling.

Your bowed mahogany chest
lists, one curly knee sunk
in rigid as steel seas
ridged like a chop tide
mirror aglare swinging
the sky.

Slid breast drawers
spill keys, sayings,
brownstained kindness,
chains.

For All the Dead

From the far sepulchres
Of our thousand generations
Are summoned here to this one ground
Hebrew song, Roman arch, Greek capital,
Baroque impassioned ordering of sound.

This high carapace, white and gilt,
Covers but cannot hide the rich
Packed dust, the stacked filth
And congregation of the dead since first
Gods thundered over earth.

All their beauty now is unfleshed,
Their wisdom slurred upon our moving lips
But in our bodies held this moment hushed
The long, long curve of time will meet
For all the dead, for us.

American Cancer Society

Although the metaphor is inert
this title takes a sidelong hold
on growing truth. We cannot
limit our concern to disease.

The nuclei alter first.

Dr. Auerbach views thousands
of slides in a few days.
E. Cuyler Hammond explains
epidemiology.

The nuclei alter first.

As in this animated diagram
Against a dull magenta ground
of normal lung cells the aberrant growth
brilliantly proliferates.

The nuclei alter first.

In the lungs, the brain, the eyes,
as in this actual shot
of a malignancy growing,
the jeweled lump, the luscious fruit,
the hoarded lapis lazuli
pulsing and glowing,
that dream of new life,
death, first birthing
in the aberrant nuclei.

This Is

          my lane
And dooryard green
Flesh garland
That the sun
Makes līve, leafs
From the ice to burn
Ash in the dust
Of my roadway down.

New Hampshire Finding*

What can you find in New Hampshire today?
Ski slopes, trailer parks, excellent highways,
maple sugar candy, mountain scenery,
fine Georgian houses under yellowing elms,
and, on the Merrimack, "the Queen City," Amoskeag,
mills, steeples, bridges, tenements, all dark brick,
"magnificent as the ruined temples of Karnak."

---

*History of the Town of Bristol, Grafton County, New Hampshire, Vol. I, *Genealogies*, Vol. II, *Annals*, by Richard W. Musgrove. Printed by R. W. Musgrove, Bristol, N.H., 1904.

The Bristol Enterprise, 1910, 1921.

A Rare Find: Ancient Spanish coins were unearthed
by Dr. C. W. Coolidge (Bristol dentist)
on his farm on the east side of the Pemigewasset.
. . . . four silver Spanish coins of the probable value
of 25¢ each, dated 1721 and 1722,
all in good condition
and one not even tarnished.
This vicinity was at the foot
of "the long carrying place," a favorite
camping place for the Indians.
Here also camped the Whites
on their expeditions against Indians in this section.

From these hills
and mountains, waters spring and well,
cut, stream and fall,
lake and river
in "natural highways": Smith, Fowler,
Cockermouth, Merrimack, Pemigewasset,
all "known to the aborigines by distinct
names. An uncertain tradition says the Indians
called this lake (Newfound)
'Pasquaney,' 'the place where birch-bark
for canoes is found.' "

The years the paper mills upstate
polluted the Pemigewasset,
a joke went round the village:
    Smellin' bad today.
    Ayah, somethin' in the lake.
    Ayah, summer folk.

In 1712 Capt. Thomas Baker's party
with a booty of Indian scalps and beaver skins
commencing the long march homeward down the
    valley
of the Pemigewasset, had reached a "poplar plain"
just south of where the Walter R. Webster
farmhouses now stand, in Bridgewater,
when they were overtaken by the Indians
lead by Waternomee, chief of the Pemigewassets.
It is said Capt. Baker and the chief
each fired at the other in the same moment.
The bullet from Waternomee's musket
grazed the cheek of Capt. Baker
as the Indian chief fell dead.

This place, high, pure and poor,
of mica-flecked granite, moss and bracken,
these palaces, maple-domed, birch-lit, spruce-spired,
balsam-sweet, hung with glassy fine pine,
never held travelers, never held settlers long.
"very full of great hills and mountains
and very rocky. Abundance
of sprus and hemlock and far and some
brch and mapols and we Campt" wrote Capt. John
    White (1725).

"One hundred years ago the Crawfords of Bridgewater
were very numerous. Thomas Crawford, later Colonel,
was the first settler within the present town limits.
Ezra Crawford, Robert Crawford, Capt. Jonathan
    Crawford
and John Crawford had large families
but the name has disappeared from the records.
Tradition says the Crawfords of Bridgewater
settled Crawfordsville, Ind.; but all efforts
to obtain information from Crawfords now living there
have been fruitless."

One hundred years after the first
Bridgewater town meeting, this pasture,
half in Bristol, half in Bridgewater,
contained the remains of thirteen farms.
Each had been the support of a large family.
The highway of stagecoach and post,
once "an avenue of Commerce," was crossed
by a stone wall. Apple and rose
gave way again to forest.

Men and women, so many early bereft, grief-struck,
work-raddled, sunstrung and swollen, ice-cracked,
huddle and thicken here like a night smoke.
Mistress Ann Bradstreet speaks through Berryman
gravely clear, but who will here do homage and record
this ragged moan of syncopated syllables?
*Ayah, hayin' weather. Cunnin' wan't he? Twan't but the
    one.*
T'others was took. Never come back. Shame.

No single voice returns but Peter Charron's, and he
came from other parts, downstate or upcountry,
came courting Will Woodward's widow and her land.
But he could tell a story, and cap in hand,
leaving his wallbuilding (he was mason, carpenter,
farmer, teamster, sometime bum), told in courtly manner
the story of his first journey to this place.
He carried a walking stick that he had cut
before setting out, and where he thrust it
into the earth, that row of poplars stands.
Oh, Peter, come back with your walking stick
and carry these spirits to rest, to earth.

The last of those folk to die on the hill was gay enough.
For years in her nineties she carried
the oldest one's gold-headed cane
of honor and, skirts tucked high,
blew down the road like a bit of fluff
every Saturday night and hitched a ride to the movies.
She and her daughter, Sarah, Peter's wife,
always had cats in a box behind the stove
and on the table fried potatoes, crullers and pie
under a cloth, and one whole room stuffed with copies
of the Bristol *Enterprise*
and a Boston paper with Sunday funnies.

The death of Frank Haynes
generally known as "Tinker" Haynes
occurred Tuesday
at the home of Andrew Phelps of Danbury.
Mr. Haynes had resided for many years
in a room of the Blake building
on So. Main St. There he slept, ate
and worked at his trade,
clock repairing, which gave him the name
"Tinker" by which he was alone known.
Much to surprise of people of Bristol
Haynes was found to be a Jew. Burial
was in Rumney.

It was the emptiness that ached,
the pure "polar pink," Henry James called it,
of new world sunsets that chilled the heart.
Was it not near this country Hawthorne caught
the loneliness no love, success
or travel ever cured? Here he dreamed of a man
for whom the Great Stone Face became
first friend, then god, then self, and of the stranger
warmed at a family hearth in White Mountain Notch
on the night a landslide killed them all.

Back from Rome, from England, "Our Old Home,"
his last steps echoed past the ranked rocking chairs
on the great white stairs and verandas
of the Pemigewasset House.
Was Hawthorne's death so near this place
another work of Maule's, of Hathorne's Curse,
"as the dreary and unprosperous condition of the race
through many a long and weary year would argue to
    exist";
was it, like Roger Malvin's, alone in the wilderness,
a legacy that exile or sacrifice
of best loved sons at last must dissipate?

Now this same emptiness shines me, hones me,
votes me, decks me, heiress of ache
in rich moss, fern and delicate grass lace,
summer's bright memory of ice,
freshes me, tunes me, primes me and sends me,
oh, sends me sad away.

How I Feel About...

Trying to Write a Poem about this Hill in New Hampshire While Staying on the Hill in New Hampshire

Almost any morning any time between three and eight
this poem that I'm trying to write
like a greedy overgrown pet
takes me in its teeth and shakes me awake
flinging snarled and gritty shreds of itself
into my sleepy head,
scaring me half sick with the ghosts it claims
I have invoked,
making me shiver and sweat and smoke
while the owls hoot too hoo
        to whom to you hoo.

If there is a lady
        muse on this mountain
she is awfully shy and refined
but there certainly are some wild beastly poems.

Sugar Maples

For Helgard

Did you know a butterfly's chrysalis
drops a scarlet afterbirth?
                        Look,
on the ground under it.
I knew the butterfly was wet, not that the wet was—
this is—brighter than blood.

We had walked up the brook, straddling the windfalls,
teetering along the stones and through the pools,
carrying our sandals, where the lumbermen—
that was already years ago—had broken the banks.
Through the new ragged poplars and hemlocks
all the way, we saw sugar maples
in groups, some cut stumps
but more standing. By contrast
they looked huge, older than God,

their pale trunks gray, white flecked
with moonspots round as dollars, bark cracked,
ravelled and pocked, branches twisted and humped
with tumors, goiters, ancient cones and craters.
     Like Majorcan olive trees, you said,
but not, like them, dryads, harpies, satyrs,
not mock human, but stout and straight,
older than God and more human.

We passed Pete's old sugar house, fallen in.
The others were all long vanished.
     Did they really use them much?
Oh, yes. Pete did, I remember. For some
it was all the sugar they had. Robert Frost
once lived on the other hill, you said,
on Bridgewater Mountain.
     How he hangs around!

The brook turned and the woodland flattened.
There seemed to be paths through the bracken.
We couldn't see light at the top of the hill
where the road should have been.
I saw your eyes had grown dreamy and green,
although your green contact lenses, I knew, were gone,
one lost, one broken.
        I thought you might stop and toe down in
to whisper out branches for a gray and green age.

When we came to the old Post road
the slope seemed longer and steeper than I remembered.
              How would you like to bowl down this
in a mail coach? I asked.
Then we saw the new butterfly
like a brown leaf on the long green grass,
a Viceroy, a Monarch-mimic, we found out later.
Above him on the grass stalk the shell poked up
blown out thin and broken at the end,
gray and stained like old plastic.

Blue Stone

The children came home from a new shop on the square
That sells only minerals—it was the paper store—
With pieces of metal and stone in plastic bags,
Low-priced, each with a neat hand-written tag:
Amber, fool's gold, rosequartz, moonstone.
The mother brought home one polished blue stone
Glued to a metal ring that would fit any finger,
A jasper pebble, irregular, gently triangular
And blue, the blue of these oldest ice-crossed,
Ice-ground and rounded mountains, shallow-bossed
Like them and veined and shaded, one corner
Black, another rimmed white, and the center,
The longest angle, blue, the blue of carpenters'
Coveralls washed out and streaked, of berries,
Ripe-bloomed, toppling into sun-struck coffee tins,
Of the plain cotton kimonos of clean-skinned
Japanese grandmothers, lively as birds and nestled
Lightly as birds in the full households

Of generous sons, those old ones, free again
As children to be merry and who move
Airily as maple keys or milkweed down carrying love
Like a seed, who have outlived all lusts
But childish lusts for sweets and dreamless rest.

Call it the worn blue stone of good old age
That the mother may wear as token and badge
Of work and harvest and love and nonsense,
Opaque and subtle as ringed old eyes, as second
    innocence.

To Alpheus Woodward...
Who Has Not Shown Up to Mow the Upper Field Which Once Belonged to His Own Grandmother

August, 1970

Something there is that doesn't love a mowing machine
and thanks to the indolence of Alpheus Woodward
this field for generations cropped stubble clean
has exploded an ebullience of berries, blue poured
into the fine gold grasses, clustered like roses,
raising blue clumps, blue thumbs, blue fists, a hoard
of greater riches between these ferns and mosses
and this blue heaven than are dreamt of, Alpheus,
in your backwoods philosophy. Count your losses,
$45 for a half day's work. Our gains are in excess
of pie and muffins; ages of gold and fable are past
and mourned, but the blue age of berries now and here
we celebrate. Good mowers may make good hay but at
    last
a lazy mower will make way for fabulous berries.